GO, GIRL

GiRL

INSPIRATION AND MOTIVATION
FOR DREAMERS, BELIEVERS
AND ACHIEVERS

summersdale

GO, GIRL

An Hachette UK Company
www.hachette.co.uk

Summersdale Publishers Ltd
Part of Octopus Publishing Group Limited
Carmelite House
50 Victoria Embankment
LONDON
EC4Y 0DZ
UK

www.summersdale.com

Printed and bound in the Czech Republic

ISBN: 978-1-78685-279-3

Substantial discounts on bulk quantities of Summersdale books are available to corporations, professional associations and other organisations. For details contact general enquiries: telephone: +44 (0) 1243 771107 or email: enquiries@summersdale.com.

TO...

FROM...

YOU HAVE A RIGHT TO BE
EXACTLY WHO YOU ARE.

MICHELLE OBAMA

TO ME,
POWER IS
MAKING
THINGS
HAPPEN
WITHOUT
ASKING FOR
PERMISSION.

BEYONCÉ

OTHER WOMEN
WHO ARE KILLING IT
SHOULD MOTIVATE
YOU, THRILL YOU,
CHALLENGE YOU AND
INSPIRE YOU.

TAYLOR SWIFT

EMPOWERED
WOMEN
EMPOWER
WOMEN.

NOURISH TO FLOURISH

If you're going to smash those goals, you need to be strong enough to do it. So take care of yourself! Make time for the little things in life, because these are the things that keep us healthy and refreshed. Eat fruit and vegetables as often as you can; try to get some fresh air every day; take time to wind down before you go to bed every night to give yourself a chance to switch off; and get a full night's sleep. It's easy to put off or forget these things when you're busy, but a little bit of self-care goes a long way.

FEEL VALIDATION OF
YOUR EXTERNAL BEAUTY,
BUT ALSO GET TO THE
DEEPER BUSINESS OF BEING
BEAUTIFUL INSIDE.

LUPITA NYONG'O

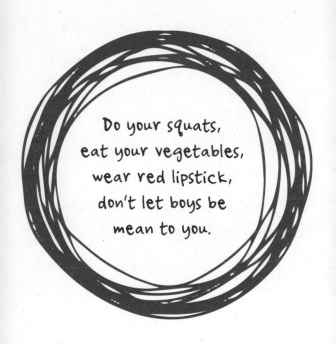

Do your squats,
eat your vegetables,
wear red lipstick,
don't let boys be
mean to you.

KENDALL JENNER

NEVER DOUBT THAT YOU ARE
VALUABLE AND POWERFUL AND
DESERVING OF EVERY CHANCE AND
OPPORTUNITY IN THE WORLD.

HILLARY CLINTON

I'M CRAZY, AND
I DON'T PRETEND TO
BE ANYTHING ELSE.

RIHANNA

i AM NOT AFRAiD TO SAY 'NO'

It might seem like putting yourself out there and saying 'yes' to everything is the best way to live a full life. But sometimes you need to know when to say 'no'. Decline the invitation for a night out if you don't really want to go. Don't take on the extra task at work if you can't actually fit it in. Saying 'no' is not a sign of weakness, nor should it be a source of guilt. In fact, saying 'no' can be incredibly empowering – it allows you to take control of your decisions and help you prioritise what's important in your life.

Do a thing called what you want.

i'M NOT iNTiMiDATED BY
HOW PEOPLE PERCEiVE ME.

DOLLY PARTON

I'M NOT THE NEXT USAIN BOLT
OR MICHAEL PHELPS.
I'M THE FIRST SIMONE BILES.

SIMONE BILES

I'M DONE COMPROMISING; EVEN MORE SO, I'M DONE WITH BEING COMPROMISED.

MILA KUNIS

ALL THE MARKS ON
THE WORLD MEAN
NOTHING COMPARED
TO THE MARKS
YOU'RE ABOUT
TO MAKE.

AMBER TAMBLYN

I AM A WOMAN – WHAT'S YOUR SUPERPOWER?

WE ARE FEARLESS

Don't be afraid to take risks. It could be something in your everyday life, such as wearing a bold red skirt, exploring a new place, or reaching out to someone who you haven't talked to for a while. Or it could be something bigger — applying for that dream job, or asking someone out on a date. Even if you start out small, make the effort to step outside your comfort zone. Once you learn how to handle the fear of doing new things, you'll be unstoppable!

YOU HAVE TO STAND FOR WHAT
YOU BELIEVE IN AND SOMETIMES
YOU HAVE TO STAND ALONE.

QUEEN LATIFAH

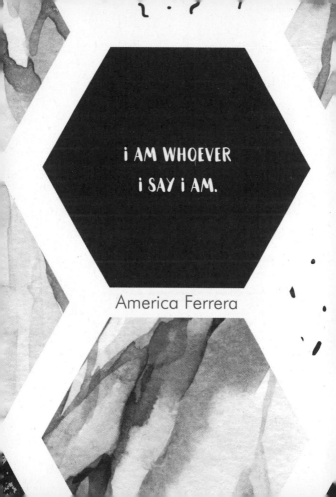

i AM WHOEVER
i SAY i AM.

America Ferrera

I do not. belong.
to anyone.
but myself.
and neither
do you.

ARIANA GRANDE

YES, I AM A FEMINIST... IT'S ABOUT OWNING YOUR POWER, EMBRACING YOUR WOMANHOOD.

ALICIA KEYS

YOU ARE NUMBER ONE

It's natural to want to please other people; in a lot of cases this can be a positive thing. But, don't let this desire become a priority. If you notice yourself repeatedly putting someone else's needs before your own, or sacrificing your own happiness for somebody else's, take a step back. While it's good to want to make the world around you a happier place, you shouldn't neglect your own well-being. It's not selfish to put yourself first — don't forget, you are the most important person in your life!

A REAL WOMAN

~~HAS CURVES~~

~~IS SKINNY~~

~~HAS MUSCLES~~

IS WHATEVER

THE HELL SHE

WANTS TO BE.

I'M OVER TRYING TO FIND THE
'ADORABLE' WAY TO STATE MY
OPINION AND STILL BE LIKABLE!

JENNIFER LAWRENCE

THE QUESTION ISN'T WHO'S
GOING TO LET ME; IT'S WHO'S
GOING TO STOP ME.

AYN RAND

WE ARE JUST
AS GREAT AS
MEN — AND
SOME OF
US CAN BE
EVEN BETTER.

LADY GAGA

KNOW WHAT?
B*TCHES GET
STUFF DONE.

TINA FEY

GREAT THINGS NEVER COME FROM THE COMFORT ZONE.

THiNK STARTING SHOT
NOT PARTING SHOT

Don't be discouraged if things get tough. Maybe reaching a goal is more difficult than you first thought. Maybe it's taking longer than you expected to see any results from your hard work. The things worth doing in life are often the hardest to achieve, so if you're finding it difficult you're probably doing it right. At times like these, think back to what made you start out in the first place. Refresh your motivation by retracing your steps back to that first spark of determination and give yourself a boost.

i STAND BY EVERY MISTAKE i'VE
EVER MADE, SO JUDGE AWAY.

KRISTEN STEWART

I don't have any limitations on what I think I could do or be.

OPRAH WINFREY

EVERY WOMAN HAS THE
RIGHT TO BECOME HERSELF,
AND DO WHATEVER
SHE NEEDS TO DO.

ANI DiFRANCO

IF YOU KNOW YOU'RE
GREAT AT WHAT YOU
DO, DON'T EVER BE
ASHAMED TO ASK
FOR THE TOP DOLLAR
IN YOUR FIELD.

NICKI MINAJ

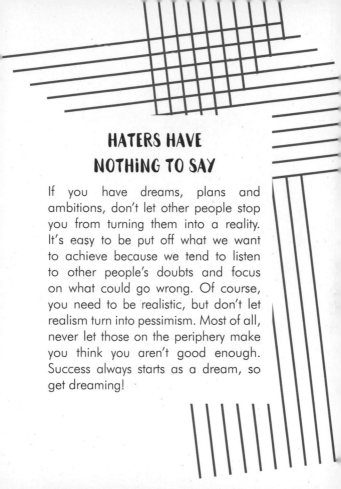

HATERS HAVE
NOTHING TO SAY

If you have dreams, plans and ambitions, don't let other people stop you from turning them into a reality. It's easy to be put off what we want to achieve because we tend to listen to other people's doubts and focus on what could go wrong. Of course, you need to be realistic, but don't let realism turn into pessimism. Most of all, never let those on the periphery make you think you aren't good enough. Success always starts as a dream, so get dreaming!

She's got that whole purpose-driven, warrior-princess, save-the-world-type vibe.

A GIRL DOESN'T NEED ANYONE
WHO DOESN'T NEED HER.

MARILYN MONROE

DON'T BE BITTER
AND MEAN COS YOU DON'T
FIT IN, IT'S A GIFT.

COURTNEY LOVE

THE MOST COURAGEOUS ACT IS STILL TO THINK FOR YOURSELF. ALOUD.

COCO CHANEL

RUN TO THE FIRE;
DON'T HIDE FROM IT.

MEG WHITMAN

STOP HOLDING BACK JUST BECAUSE THE OTHERS CAN'T KEEP UP.

SHE BELIEVED SHE COULD, SO SHE DID

Sometimes the difference between making your dreams a reality and leaving them as figments of your imagination comes down to self-belief. This sounds like a small thing, but it's far from it: it's what motivates you to start and it will keep you going through the tougher times. If you're starting out, try setting a small goal first to prove to yourself that *you can* – write 500 words of that novel, or run a mile of the marathon, for example. If you're midway through a project, remind yourself of how far you've already come!

A LOT OF PEOPLE ARE AFRAID
TO SAY WHAT THEY WANT.
THAT'S WHY THEY DON'T
GET WHAT THEY WANT.

MADONNA

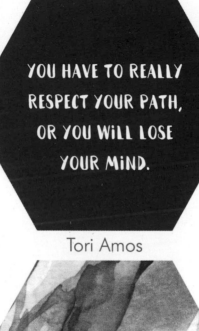

YOU HAVE TO REALLY
RESPECT YOUR PATH,
OR YOU WILL LOSE
YOUR MIND.

Tori Amos

THiS BODY HAS ENABLED ME
TO BE THE GREATEST PLAYER
i CAN BE, AND i'M NOT GOING
TO SCRUTiNiSE THAT.

SERENA WiLLIAMS

IF WE ARE UNITED, THERE IS NO LIMIT TO WHAT WE CAN DO.

AMAL CLOONEY

KiNDNESS iS KEY

If you wouldn't say it to your best friend, then don't say it to yourself. When things don't go quite to plan, criticising yourself will only fill you with negative feelings. This won't make things better, nor will it motivate you to carry on. Instead, try to be constructive and work on a way to see the situation from a more positive perspective. For instance, you haven't failed – it just hasn't worked this time. Don't be afraid to give yourself another chance. With kindness and respect, you'll get to where you want to be!

SHE WASN'T LOOKING FOR A KNIGHT. SHE WAS LOOKING FOR A SWORD.

I'M DONE WITH BEING PASSIVE
ABOUT ANY KIND OF STATUS QUO
THAT ALLOWS ANYONE TO SUFFER
OR TO BE DISRESPECTED.

GRIMES

WITHOUT LEAPS OF
IMAGINATION, OR DREAMING,
WE LOSE THE EXCITEMENT OF
POSSIBILITIES. DREAMING, AFTER
ALL, IS A FORM OF PLANNING.

GLORIA STEINEM

YOU CHANGE THE WORLD BY BEING YOURSELF.

YOKO ONO

THE BEAUTY OF
BEING A FEMINIST
IS THAT YOU GET TO
BE WHATEVER YOU
WANT, AND THAT'S
THE POINT.

SHONDA RHIMES

STOP WAITING AND GET WHAT'S YOURS.

SHOUT OUT FOR THE SQUAD

Being strong doesn't have to mean being alone. Knowing when to ask for help is one of the most valuable skills you can learn. If you need advice, a favour, or even just someone to talk to, try reaching out and you might be surprised – most of the time, people will want to help you, especially your family and friends. You may even find that collaborating gives you a chance to strengthen your friendships with the people around you, as you share in what you're doing.

GIRLS GOT BALLS. THEY'RE
JUST A LITTLE HIGHER UP.

JOAN JETT

I wouldn't do anything, I wouldn't work anywhere, if I wasn't interested in getting to the very top.

JESS PHILLIPS

YOU ARE VALUED, YOU
ARE A GODDESS AND
DON'T FORGET THAT.

JENNIFER LOPEZ

IT'S NOT ABOUT BEING
THE PRETTIEST IN THE
CLASS – IT'S WHAT
YOU DO IN THE CLASS.

VICTORIA BECKHAM

THROW ME TO THE WOLVES AND i WiLL RETURN LEADiNG THE PACK

If you find yourself in a stressful situation, whether it's at work or at home, don't let it spin you into a panic. First, remain positive. Tell yourself 'I can', rather than 'I can't'. Try to put spiralling thoughts of 'what if…?' to one side, too. Focus instead on what is in front of you right now – this will help you to keep a handle on your emotions, maintain a clear head and let you focus on making a plan so you can deal with the situation calmly and confidently. No sweat.

Own who
you are.

NEVER FEAR BEING
VULGAR, ONLY BORING.

DIANA VREELAND

A BOSSY WOMAN iS
SOMEONE TO SEARCH
OUT AND TO CELEBRATE.

AMY POEHLER

YOU ARE COMPLEX,
AND YOU ARE
MULTIDIMENSIONAL.
THE SOONER YOU START
TO EMBRACE THAT, THE
SOONER YOU'LL BE OK
WITH YOURSELF.

RASHIDA JONES

WE GET TO DECIDE
FOR OURSELVES
WHAT IS BEAUTIFUL
WHEN IT COMES TO
OUR BODIES. THAT
DECISION IS OURS AND
OURS ALONE.

JENNIFER ANISTON

NEVER APOLOGISE FOR BEING A POWERFUL WOMAN.

YOU ARE ENOUGH

You, just as you are, are enough. You are worthy of happiness, love and peace – and no matter where life takes you, you always will be. This doesn't mean that you will never grow and change, or that you will never make mistakes. But it does mean that, whatever happens, you're complete just the way you are. So follow your aspirations wherever they may take you and know that there is no need to prove yourself. Accept yourself for everything you are – imperfections and all – because you are you, and that is enough.

FIND OUT WHO YOU ARE
AND BE THAT PERSON.

ELLEN DeGENERES

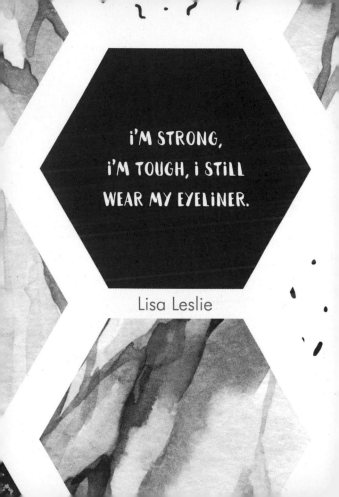

i'M STRONG,
i'M TOUGH, i STiLL
WEAR MY EYELiNER.

Lisa Leslie

YOU HAVE TO BELIEVE
IN YOURSELF WHEN
NO ONE ELSE DOES
– THAT MAKES
YOU A WINNER
RIGHT THERE.

VENUS WILLIAMS

IF YOU DON'T
LIKE THE ROAD
YOU'RE WALKING,
START PAVING
ANOTHER ONE.

DOLLY PARTON

GOOD-VIBE TRIBE

The people you choose to spend your time with have a huge impact on you — from your sense of humour, to the decisions you make. If you feel that someone consistently belittles you, or drains your energy, don't feel obliged to spend your time with them; you don't need that kind of negativity dragging you down. Put your own needs first and distance yourself from them. Instead, surround yourself with people who lift you up, support your ambitions and bring out your best side. Good vibes only!

NEVERTHELESS,
SHE PERSISTED.

THE ONLY ONE WHO CAN TELL YOU
'YOU CAN'T WIN' IS YOU, AND YOU
DON'T HAVE TO LISTEN.

JESSICA ENNIS-HILL

WE CAN BE THE CHANGE WE WANT
TO SEE. LET'S GO, LET'S HAVE AN
AGENDA, AND LET'S DO THIS.

ROSE McGOWAN

I REMIND
MYSELF TO
BE KIND
TO MYSELF.

EMMA STONE

WHO CARES?
DO YOUR THING,
AND DON'T CARE IF
THEY LIKE IT.

TINA FEY

REAL QUEENS FIX EACH OTHER'S CROWNS.

MY BODY, MY RULES

Dye your hair; get a tattoo; pierce your ears; wear clashing colours – or not! Dress yourself in what makes *you* feel good, whether that's 6-inch heels or your scruffiest trainers. Don't worry about what other people will think, and don't tone yourself down to please someone else. The only thing that matters is that you feel confident and comfortable. It's OK to dress for the occasion (hot pants and thigh-high boots might not be considered suitable work attire), but don't curb your style to keep other people happy.

BE YOURSELF. DO WHATEVER YOU
WANT TO DO AND DON'T LET
BOUNDARIES HOLD YOU BACK.

SOPHIE TURNER

If you set your
mind to something,
you can accomplish
that and then some.

SARAH HYLAND

GET TO KNOW YOURSELF
BEFORE YOU LET ANYONE
ELSE INTO YOUR PARTY.

ALLISON JANNEY

I AM NOT A
HAS-BEEN.
I AM A
WILL BE.

LAUREN BACALL

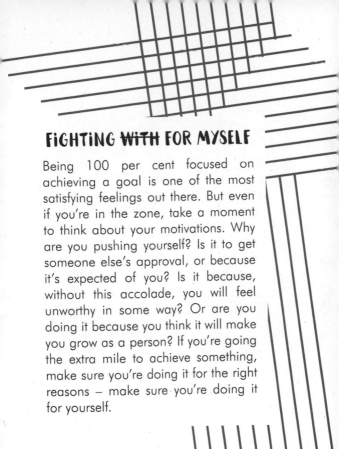

FiGHTiNG ~~WiTH~~ FOR MYSELF

Being 100 per cent focused on achieving a goal is one of the most satisfying feelings out there. But even if you're in the zone, take a moment to think about your motivations. Why are you pushing yourself? Is it to get someone else's approval, or because it's expected of you? Is it because, without this accolade, you will feel unworthy in some way? Or are you doing it because you think it will make you grow as a person? If you're going the extra mile to achieve something, make sure you're doing it for the right reasons – make sure you're doing it for yourself.

Be you.
Do you.
For you.

DIFFERENT IS GOOD.

SERENA WILLIAMS

A DAME THAT KNOWS
THE ROPES ISN'T LIKELY
TO GET TIED UP.

MAE WEST

IF YOU LOOK CONFIDENT
YOU CAN PULL OFF
ANYTHING, EVEN IF YOU
HAVE NO CLUE WHAT
YOU'RE DOING.

JESSICA ALBA

STICKING UP FOR
OURSELVES IN THE
SAME WAY WE
WOULD ONE OF OUR
FRIENDS IS A HARD
BUT SATISFYING
THING TO DO.

AMY POEHLER

GRL PWR.

i'M SMiLiNG 'CAUSE i GOT THiS

You've heard the phrase, 'you've got to fake it to make it' – it may sound silly, but it's true. Whatever you're feeling inside, whether you're shy, scared, sad or unsure, try putting on a brave face, even if it's only for a few minutes. Hold your head up, stand tall and smile. Present yourself like someone who has all the confidence in the world; someone who would tell themselves, 'I've got this'. Keep it up and pretty soon you won't be pretending any more because, girl, you *have* got this.

MAKING BAD DECISIONS DOESN'T
MAKE YOU A BAD PERSON.
IT IS HOW YOU LEARN TO
MAKE BETTER CHOICES.

DREW BARRYMORE

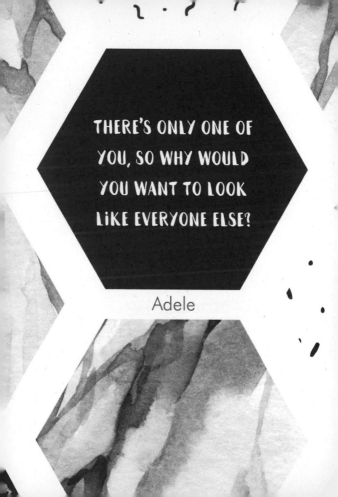

THERE'S ONLY ONE OF YOU, SO WHY WOULD YOU WANT TO LOOK LIKE EVERYONE ELSE?

Adele

THAT IS PROBABLY THE BEST
WAY TO FEEL CONFIDENT ABOUT
YOURSELF – BE GRATEFUL AND
HAPPY FOR YOUR LOT.

FEARNE COTTON

IF SOMEONE HAS
GOT A PROBLEM
WITH A SIZE-12 GIRL
WALKING IN WITH NO
MAKE-UP ON... THAT'S
THEIR ISSUE.

CHARLOTTE CHURCH

PUTTING ON THE WAR PAINT

We all have times when we need an extra boost of confidence. Sometimes, the little things are all it takes to help you look today in the eye. Do you have a big meeting today? Then wear that bold lipstick that you love. Going to an event where you don't know many people? Good thing you've got that killer outfit! Do whatever you need to do to make yourself feel good so you can conquer whatever your day has in store for you with confidence.

SOMETIMES IT'S
THE PRINCESS
WHO SLAYS
THE DRAGON
AND SAVES
THE PRINCE.

i LOVE TO SEE A YOUNG GiRL
GO OUT AND GRAB THE
WORLD BY THE LAPELS.

MAYA ANGELOU

IT'S OK TO BE POWERFUL
IN EVERY WAY: TO BE BIG,
TO TAKE UP SPACE.
TO BREATHE AND THRIVE.

CLAIRE DANES

I CAN'T THINK OF ANY BETTER REPRESENTATION OF BEAUTY THAN SOMEONE WHO IS UNAFRAID TO BE HERSELF.

EMMA STONE

PASSION IS ENERGY.
FEEL THE POWER
THAT COMES FROM
FOCUSING ON WHAT
EXCITES YOU.

OPRAH WINFREY

BE THE GAME CHANGER.

DREAM iT, THEN DO iT

Don't be afraid to go after something that seems unrealistic now. Remember that every expert, professional or master of their field, was once a beginner too — we all have to start somewhere. We grow by doing new things, challenging ourselves and pushing ourselves to step slightly out of our comfort zones, so if you have an ambition, pursue it! You never know where it might lead or what new opportunities it will open up for you.

THERE IS NO SHAME IN
BEING A BOSS.

KATY PERRY

I didn't get there
by wishing for it or
hoping for it, but
by working for it.

ESTÉE LAUDER

CHERISH FOREVER WHAT
MAKES YOU UNIQUE, 'CUZ YOU'RE
REALLY A YAWN IF IT GOES.

BETTE MIDLER

WHEN I'M TIRED,
I REST. I SAY,
'I CAN'T BE A
SUPERWOMAN
TODAY.'

JADA PINKETT SMITH

LEARN TO REST,
NOT TO QUIT

You don't have to be on your A-game all the time. Allow yourself to switch off and give yourself room to rest if you're having trouble with something. Whether it's a particular problem you can't think your way around, or you're having an off-day and you're struggling to find energy, more often than not, a break is all you'll need to get back on track. Everybody needs some time off once in a while, so take a breather! You can return later with a fresher mind.

YOU HAVE WHAT iT TAKES TO BE
A ViCTORiOUS, iNDEPENDENT,
FEARLESS WOMAN.

TYRA BANKS

MY COACH SAID i RAN LiKE
A GiRL, i SAiD iF HE RAN A
LiTTLE FASTER HE COULD TOO.

MIA HAMM

OUGHT NOT EVERY WOMAN, LIKE EVERY MAN, TO FOLLOW THE BENT OF HER OWN TALENTS?

ANNE LOUISE GERMAINE DE STAËL

IT'S NOT YOUR JOB TO LIKE ME, IT'S MINE.

BYRON KATIE

FIGHT LIKE A GIRL.

WOMEN'S RIGHTS ARE HUMAN RIGHTS

We all have patterns that we fall into, and sometimes this makes it hard to notice when we're letting gender politics affect us. Watch your behaviour in certain situations or in the presence of particular people. Do you avoid confrontation or speaking up because you're afraid of being 'bossy' or too forward? If it was a man speaking out, or going against the grain, does the situation change in any way? Don't be afraid to call out sexism when you see it, and to stand up for others when you see it affecting them. Your worth is not determined by your gender.

LOVE YOURSELF FIRST
AND EVERYTHING ELSE
FALLS INTO LINE.

LUCILLE BALL

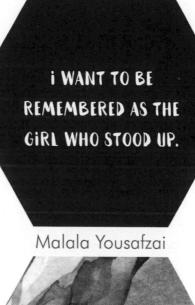

i WANT TO BE REMEMBERED AS THE GiRL WHO STOOD UP.

Malala Yousafzai

FEET, WHAT DO i NEED
YOU FOR WHEN i HAVE
WiNGS TO FLY?

FRIDA KAHLO

I'VE BEEN THROUGH
IT ALL, BABY, I'M
MOTHER COURAGE.

ELIZABETH TAYLOR

LET iT OUT

Anger is not a 'bad' emotion. Sometimes, it can be the right response to a situation – possibly even the healthiest one, too! So if you're really riled up, frustrated, offended or distressed by something that's been said or done, don't try to hide it. Talk to someone about how you're feeling. Confront the root of the problem. Or just scream and cry into a pillow. Whatever you do, don't bottle it up! It's OK to cry and it's all right to be angry, just as long as you don't let it stop you from doing your thing.

LIFE IS TOUGH,
BUT, DARLING,
SO ARE YOU.

DON'T COMPROMISE YOURSELF.
YOU ARE ALL YOU'VE GOT.

JANIS JOPLIN

THE MOST EFFECTIVE WAY
TO DO IT, IS TO DO IT.

AMELIA EARHART

BUCKLE UP, AND KNOW THAT IT'S GOING TO BE A TREMENDOUS AMOUNT OF WORK, BUT EMBRACE IT.

TORY BURCH

NEVER GROW
A WISHBONE,
DAUGHTER, WHERE
YOUR BACKBONE
OUGHT TO BE.

CLEMENTINE PADDLEFORD

SHE
NEEDED
A HERO,
SO THAT'S
WHAT SHE
BECAME.

WE ARE ALL WONDER WOMEN

Everybody has something they're good at. It could be a hobby or a skill, like art or a sport; maybe it's something in your personality, like being able to keep a cool head in a crisis or being a good listener. It could even be something small, like always remembering when people's birthdays are. Whatever your many and varied talents, cherish them! Celebrate your skills and be proud of what you can do, because it's what makes you the amazing individual that you are.

THE BEST PROTECTION
ANY WOMAN CAN
HAVE IS COURAGE.

ELIZABETH CADY STANTON

Whatever you have conquered, it shines through your mind.

NIKKI ROWE

ACCEPT NOTHING BUT THE
FACT THAT YOU'RE EQUAL.

NEKO CASE

BEING A ROCKSTAR IS NOT A BOY'S GAME.

BRANDI CARLILE

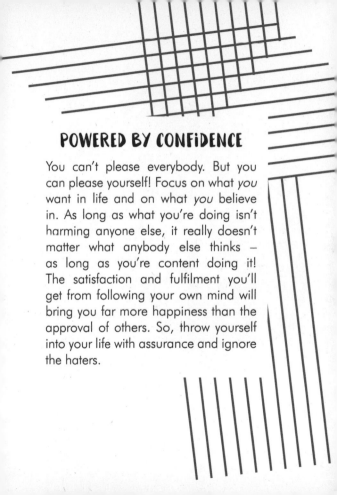

POWERED BY CONFIDENCE

You can't please everybody. But you can please yourself! Focus on what *you* want in life and on what *you* believe in. As long as what you're doing isn't harming anyone else, it really doesn't matter what anybody else thinks – as long as you're content doing it! The satisfaction and fulfilment you'll get from following your own mind will bring you far more happiness than the approval of others. So, throw yourself into your life with assurance and ignore the haters.

Girl almighty.

NEVER, NEVER, NEVER
GIVE UP. AND REMEMBER
TO DANCE A LITTLE.

GLORIA STEINEM

IT'S GOOD TO BREAK THE
MOULD AND RECREATE ONE.

KIM KARDASHIAN

IT ISN'T WHERE
YOU CAME FROM,
IT'S WHERE
YOU'RE GOING
THAT COUNTS.

ELLA FITZGERALD

YOU DON'T LUCK
INTO INTEGRITY.
YOU WORK AT IT.

BETTY WHITE

I LOVE THE PERSON I'VE BECOME BECAUSE I'VE FOUGHT TO BECOME HER.

iT'S NEVER TOO LATE

If you've been working towards a goal for a long time, it can feel as if you're duty-bound to continue. But whatever stage you're at — whether you're five weeks into a project or five years — remember that you can always change direction if the direction you're headed is no longer working for you. Or you could turn around and go all the way back to the beginning and start afresh: it's never too late to start again. Your time is precious, so don't waste it doing something you're not passionate about.

i DON'T TRY TO SOUND
LiKE ANYONE BUT ME.

NORAH JONES

NO ONE CAN FIGURE
OUT YOUR WORTH
BUT YOU.

Betty Carter

ALWAYS BE A FIRST-RATE
VERSION OF YOURSELF, INSTEAD
OF A SECOND-RATE VERSION
OF SOMEBODY ELSE.

JUDY GARLAND

YOU HAVE GOT TO DISCOVER YOU, WHAT YOU DO, AND TRUST IT.

BARBRA STREISAND

TRUST AND BELIEVE, BABE

If you don't believe in yourself and your convictions then other people won't be convinced either. Trust your ideas and opinions and share them confidently. If you are presenting a topic publicly — perhaps at an interview, at a meeting or in a presentation — try to speak slowly and calmly even if you are feeling the opposite inside. Try to make eye contact with everyone you are addressing in order to create a sense of intimacy among the group. Go out there, speak from the heart and show them how it's done!

BADASS

BABES

CLUB.

THINK LIKE A QUEEN.
A QUEEN IS NOT AFRAID TO FAIL.
FAILURE IS ANOTHER STEPPING
STONE TO GREATNESS.

OPRAH WINFREY

YOU HAVE TO BELIEVE
IN YOURSELF OR
NO ONE ELSE WILL.

SARAH MICHELLE GELLAR

DEFINE SUCCESS
ON YOUR OWN
TERMS, ACHIEVE
IT BY YOUR
OWN RULES,
AND BUILD
A LIFE YOU'RE
PROUD TO LIVE.

ANNE SWEENEY

YOU DON'T HAVE TO
HAVE MAGIC UNICORN
POWERS. YOU WORK
AT IT, AND YOU
GET BETTER.

KATHLEEN HANNA

I DIDN'T COME THIS FAR TO ONLY COME THIS FAR.

YOU'RE KILLING IT!

If you're pushing yourself towards a particular goal, you're sure to have both good days and not-so-good days. If you feel like things aren't going your way, don't worry. Progress isn't a smooth and steady thing; it's natural to have moments of doubt, or times when you feel like things are against you. Try not to let these times get you down. Sacrifices, setbacks, struggles – they're all part of the progress that you're making towards your goal. Have faith that you're doing a good job, even though it might not feel like it all the time. You're killing it!

DON'T WORK OUT BECAUSE
YOU THINK YOU 'NEED' TO.
DO IT BECAUSE YOUR BODY
DESERVES LOVE, RESPECT
AND HEALTHY ATTENTION.

DEMI LOVATO

I am the person
I know best.

FRIDA KAHLO

WHY DO SOME PEOPLE SAY 'GROW
SOME BALLS'? BALLS ARE WEAK
AND SENSITIVE. IF YOU WANNA
BE TOUGH, GROW A VAGINA.

BETTY WHITE

I GOT MY OWN BACK.

MAYA ANGELOU

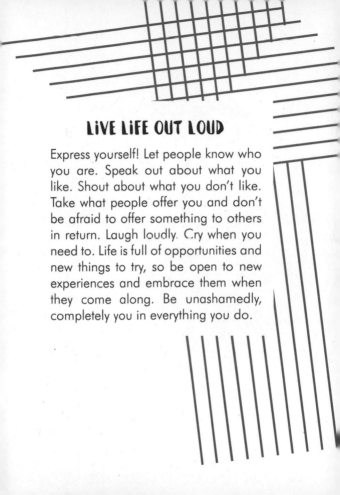

LIVE LIFE OUT LOUD

Express yourself! Let people know who you are. Speak out about what you like. Shout about what you don't like. Take what people offer you and don't be afraid to offer something to others in return. Laugh loudly. Cry when you need to. Life is full of opportunities and new things to try, so be open to new experiences and embrace them when they come along. Be unashamedly, completely you in everything you do.

She's a little sass and a lot of badass.

i WANT TO BE RESPECTED
iN ALL OF MY FEMALENESS
BECAUSE i DESERVE TO BE.

CHIMAMANDA NGOZI ADICHIE

If you're interested in finding out more about our books, find us on Facebook at **Summersdale Publishers** and follow us on Twitter at @Summersdale.

www.summersdale.com